Today is a Sunny Day

by Martha E. H. Rustad

raintree

a Capstone company — publishers for children

Raintree is an imprint of Capstone Global Library Limited, a company incorporated in England and Wales having its registered office at 264 Banbury Road, Oxford, OX2 7DY – Registered company number: 6695582

www.raintree.co.uk
myorders@raintree.co.uk

Edited by Marissa Kirkman
Designed by Charmaine Whitman and Peggie Carley
Picture research by Tracey Engel
Production by Katy LaVigne
Originated by Capstone Global Library
Printed and bound in China.

ISBN 978 1 4747 3873 6
20 19 18 17 16
10 9 8 7 6 5 4 3 2 1

British Library Cataloguing in Publication Data
A full catalogue record for this book is available from the British Library.

Acknowledgements
We would like to thank the following for permission to reproduce photographs: iStockphoto: Christopher Futcher, 8 (top), 20, karelnoppe, cover; Shutterstock: Aleksey Vanin, 6 (weather icons), Ferdiperdozniy, 12 (sun icons); goja1, cover and interior design element, Gazlast, 6 (map), JPC-PROD, 1, 18, katarina_1, 12 (children), Kseniia Neverkovska, cover and interior design element, Pakhnyushchy, 10, Sergey Novikov, 8 (bottom), Smileus, 16, Triff, 4, Zurijeta, 14

Every effort has been made to contact copyright holders of material reproduced in this book. Any omissions will be rectified in subsequent printings if notice is given to the publisher.

Contents

What is the weather like?

Today is a sunny day.

The sun is shining.

There are not many clouds

in the sky to block the sun.

Let's find out more about the weather.

Today's forecast

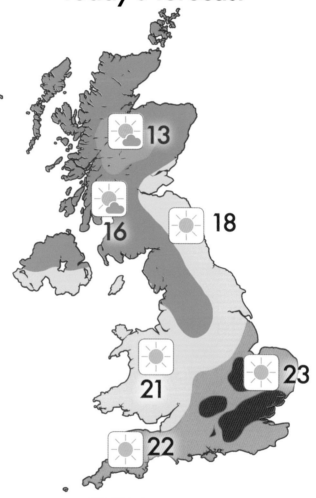

Today's forecast tells us it will be sunny.

The numbers tell us the temperatures.

A small number means it will be cold.

It will be warm if we see a big number.

summer

winter

Forecasts show patterns.

The sun can shine for several days.

Sunny days are warm in spring

and summer. Sunny days are

cool in autumn and winter.

What do we see?

The sun gives us light.

We see the sun's rays in the blue sky.

The light from the sun is all around.

N
W —|— E
S

Sunrise	Noon	Sunset

| We see the sunrise in the east. | We see the sun overhead at noon. | We see the sunset in the west. |

It looks like the sun moves in the sky.

But the sun does not move.

As the Earth spins, the sun appears
to move across the sky. Sunrise is
in the east. Sunset is in the west.

We see our shadows on the ground.

Our shadows look long in the morning.

At noon, our shadows are very short.

In the afternoon, they are long again.

What do we do?

The sun gives Earth heat and light.

Heat from the sun warms the air.

We can use sunlight to make electricity.

Solar panels gather sunlight

all year long.

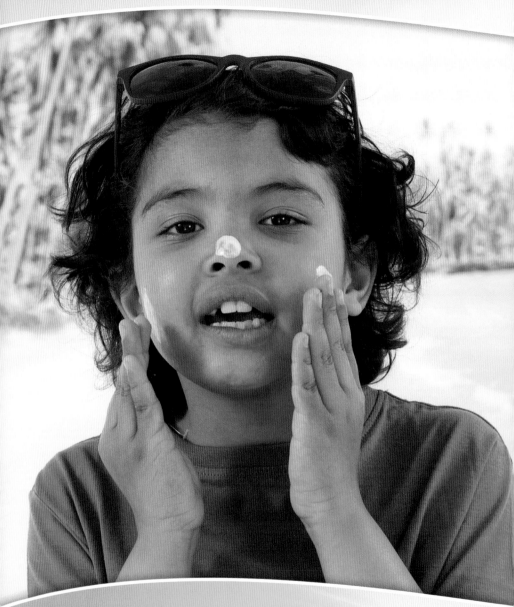

Too much time in the sun

can hurt our skin. We protect

our skin with sun cream.

We wear sunglasses, too.

The bright sun can hurt our eyes.

We work in the garden

on a sunny summer day.

Plants need sunlight to grow.

Will it be sunny again tomorrow?

Let's check the forecast.

Glossary

electricity a form of energy

forecast prediction of what the weather will be

garden small area of land where people grow food or flowers

pattern several things that are repeated in the same way each time

shadow dark area caused by blocking light

solar panel tool that gathers sunlight and turns it into electricity

sunrise time in the morning when the sun first appears

sun cream lotion that keeps skin safe from harmful parts of sunshine

sunset time at night when the sun disappears

temperature the measured heat or cold of something; temperature is measured with a thermometer

Find out more

Books

Light (Science in a Flash), Georgia Amson-Bradshaw (Franklin Watts, 2017)

Solar Energy (Alternative Energy), Kate Conley (Core Library, 2016)

Sunshine (Weather Wise), Helen Cox Cannons (Raintree, 2015)

Websites

www.eia.gov/kids/energy.cfm?page=solar_home-basics
Learn about solar energy and how solar power works.

www.peepandthebigwideworld.com/en/educators/
curriculum/center-based-educators/shadows/activity/
stand-alone/519/trace-your-shadow
Visit this site to find directions to trace your shadow.

spaceplace.nasa.gov/seasons/en
Learn how Earth's movement causes seasons.

Index

Note to parents and teachers

The What is the Weather Today? series supports National Curriculum requirements for science related to weather. This book describes and illustrates a sunny day. The images support early readers in understanding the text. The repetition of words and phrases helps early readers learn new words. This book also introduces early readers to subject-specific vocabulary words, which are defined in the Glossary section. Early readers may need assistance to read some words and to use the Contents, Glossary, Find out more and Index sections of the book.